ATE DUE

0

Cities through Time

Daily Life in
Ancient and Modern
LONDON

by Betony Toht and David Toht

illustrations by Ray Webb

ᚱᚹ

Runestone Press/Minneapolis
An imprint of Lerner Publishing Group

The *Cities through Time* series is produced by Runestone Press, an imprint of Lerner Publishing Group, in cooperation with Greenleaf Publishing, Inc., Geneva, Illinois.

Text design by Melanie Lawson, Jean DeVaty, and Rebecca JonMichaels. Cover design by Michael Tacheny.

Runestone Press
An imprint of Lerner Publishing Group
241 First Avenue North
Minneapolis, Minnesota 55401 U.S.A.

Website address: www.lernerbooks.com

Library of Congress Cataloging-in-Publication Data

Toht, Betony.
Toht, David.
     Daily life in ancient and modern London / by Betony Toht and David Toht; illustrations by Ray Webb.
          p. cm. — (Cities through Time)
     Includes index.
     Summary: Describes daily life in London from the time of the Roman invasion in A.D. 43, through medieval, Elizabethan, and Victorian times, on to the reign of Elizabeth II.
     ISBN 0-8225-3223-9 (lib. bdg.: alk. paper)
     I. Title. II. Series. III. Webb, Ray, ill. 1. London (England)—Social life and customs—Juvenile literature. 2. London (England)—History—Juvenile literature. [1. London (England)]
     DA688 .T64 2001
     942.1—dc21   99-006874

Manufactured in the United States of America
1 2 3 4 5 6 – JR – 06 05 04 03 02 01

Contents

Introduction

Few cities are as famous as London, and few cities can claim so many contributions to the world. When writer Samuel Johnson said, "When you are tired of London, you are tired of life," he captured London's limitless capacity to fascinate.

London's Bronze Age beginnings are hidden beneath the layers of the city's history. Even the Celtic-language origins of its name are buried. London may have gotten its name from Llyn-din (meaning "fort on the lake"), Llhwdinas (town among the woods), Lhongdinas (town of ships), or Luan-din (city of the moon).

From the beginning, London's location made it a trading center. The mouth of the Thames River, some forty winding miles away from London, is separated from the entrance of the Rhine (an important European river) by just over one hundred miles of choppy English Channel. A ship could load up with cheese, wine, and spices in mainland Europe and head to London almost entirely on sheltered river. Where the deepwater tidal river mellows into a placid waterway, the ship's crew could find gravel banks that made for easy unloading. Carts and pack

animals could then carry goods into the countryside.

As the centuries passed, scholars, clerics, architects, and musicians arrived, bringing new ideas and inventions. Eventually, London's position as a world-class port city attracted not only European visitors but also travelers from Africa, Asia, and the Americas. Many settled in London, making it an ethnically diverse and fascinating city of modern times.

The Houses of Parliament, Big Ben, Saint Paul's Cathedral, and Tower Bridge form a stunning backdrop to London's Thames River *(below)*. A horseguard *(left)* at his post along Whitehall is a familiar part of a city rich in traditions.

Londinium

Celtic tribes, led by powerful chiefs, ruled in England for centuries. In the area of modern-day London, the Celtic people built large hill forts to protect their farms from other nations. These forts were strong, but they proved no match for the Roman invasion that came during the first century A.D.

With a force of reluctant soldiers who thought they were going to the ends of the world, the Roman army of Emperor Claudius invaded Britain in A.D. 43. Claudius quickly saw the possibilities of what he called "Londinium" and floated a pontoon bridge across the Thames.

The Romans knew how to build cities. They laid out gravel streets, piped in fresh water through hollowed-out elm logs, and dug drains. At first, the buildings were made of wood, plaster, and straw.

Traders set up shop, delivering pottery, wine, olive oil, grain, and even glass to the new Roman forts in and near Londinium. But the boomtown itself was not well protected. When the people of the Iceni nation, led by Queen Boudicca, rebelled against Rome in A.D. 60, the city was burned to the ground. The Romans responded by savagely defeating the Iceni.

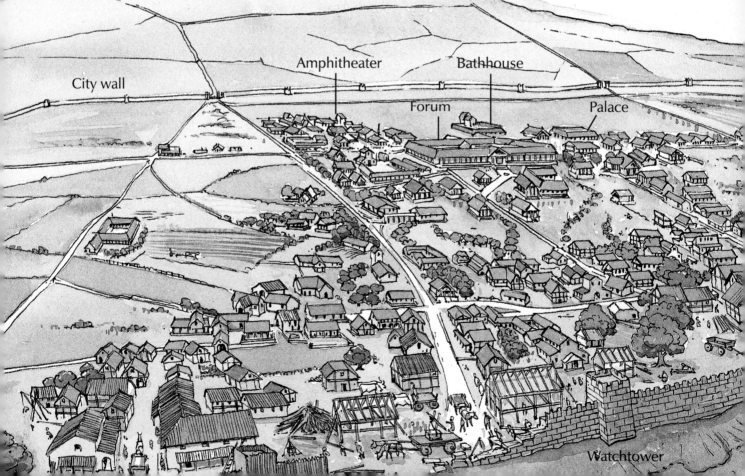

City wall

Amphitheater

Forum

Bathhouse

Palace

Watchtower

They then rebuilt their city with brick and stone. Soon residents had a forum (marketplace), a small temple, an ornate governor's palace, a garrison, an amphitheater, and public bathhouses.

Many Londoners adopted Roman habits. Some even taught their children Latin, the Roman language. Many wore loose-fitting clothes called togas. They ate Roman fish sauces, made by packing fish and spices in a jar and letting the mixture rot until it became liquid.

Middle-class Londoners lived in brick houses covered with stucco and painted deep red. Intricate mosaics made from small, brightly colored pieces of tile decorated the insides of the houses.

Some buildings were four or five stories tall, with a garden courtyard in the center. Some even had a hypocaust: an under-floor heating system.

Thousands of slaves lived in Londinium. mostly in wood-and-plaster houses with dirt floors. They kept warm over small fireplaces. Little cooking was done in these houses. Instead, slaves and other city dwellers bought bread, soup, and stews from nearby shops. Working people had little time off and, like laborers everywhere, resented lazy coworkers. One anonymous worker tattled on a colleague by scratching on a tile: "For the past thirteen days, Autalis has gone off on his own."

Bridge

Garrison

Temples

The Romans built a bridge near the modern-day sites of the Houses of Parliament and Big Ben.

Wharf

7

A British City

About A.D. 200, the Romans built a wall around London to protect the people who lived in the city. But the Celtic people and foreign invaders who threatened London were still at the gate. To raise money to defend its empire, Rome heavily taxed the citizens of London. When the Roman Empire fell in the fifth century, London was without military protection and was drained of funds. London was left to fend for itself.

No longer a boomtown and threatened by invading Jutes and Saxons, the city slowly declined into an oversized rural village. Weeds grew in once busy streets, and dirt filled the drainage ditches. Locals took apart fine Roman buildings. People used the bricks and stones to build more humble dwellings.

But London was still a trading center. The city's merchants dealt in local goods, such as grain, slaves, and most important, wool. Without Rome to impose its culture, London began to develop an identity of its own. Scandinavian and Germanic peoples invaded England but appear to have never sacked London. Instead the newcomers settled on its outskirts. They added to the town's diverse mixture of people, which included Gauls, Italians, Spaniards, North Africans, and Danubians.

Slave markets were a common sight on London streets.

Merchants transported large quantities of grain and wool.

9

Watchtowers protected by roofs

Watchtowers protected by roofs

Masons prepared stones.

Th White Tow r

In 1066 the Normans (a group from Normandy in northern France) invaded southeastern England. Led by William, duke of Normandy, the Normans seized control of England at the Battle of Hastings. From then on, William was known as William the Conqueror. He was crowned king of England in Westminster Abbey in the center of London. William the Conqueror faced an uneasy succession to the throne. Powerful people at home and abroad challenged his right to rule. To celebrate his victory and to protect England against invaders, he proposed building a massive fortress.

The fort was built on the hill where, years before, Queen Boudicca had fought against the Romans. This location was a prime lookout post, and the banks of the Thames River provided natural protection against invaders. The remains of thick Roman walls were also on the hill, giving the fort even more protection.

Gundulf, a pious and capable French monk, was chosen as the architect. He planned for thick walls to be made out of heavy limestone. Red Roman bricks, pounded to a powder, were also used, causing one observer to believe the building had been "built with mortars tempered with the blood of beasts."

Long, narrow slit windows kept the arrows of attackers from entering the fort but still allowed the fort's inhabitants to shoot arrows out. The whitewashed building loomed over the wooden town and was an imposing presence. Called the White Tower, it came to be known as the Tower of London.

The White Tower was like a city within the city. Not only a wartime stronghold, it was a home, a zoo, a place of worship, and a prison. The inner walls held herb and spice gardens and canvas and wooden housing for servants, soldiers, and craftspeople. Exotic animals whined restlessly as musicians practiced, as meat sizzled in preparation for luncheon feasts, and as hundreds of people went about their daily business.

Remains of Roman fort

Delights of the City

During medieval times (A.D. 450 to A.D. 1500), Londoners woke to roosters crowing, horse hooves clattering on the cobblestones, and sheep bleating on their way to Smithfield Market. Breakfast consisted of bread, cheese, and watered-down beer. Milk was rare, and tea and coffee were then unknown in England. A warning shout and a splash meant that someone had dumped a chamber pot, full of human waste, from an upstairs window. Scavenging hawks squawked and circled in the air. The smells of raw sewage and rotting meat from butcher shops overpowered the more pleasant smell of fresh bread. Over it all hung the smell of damp straw and wood smoke.

During Lent (a time of fasting before Easter), viewers enjoyed horse races and mock battles. On Easter, boys rowed

> *There is in London upon the river's bank, amid the wine that is sold from ship and wine-cellars, a public cookshop. There daily, according to the season, you may find viands [a variety of foods], dishes roast, fired and boiled, fish great and small, the coarser flesh for the poor, the more delicate for the rich, such as venison and birds both big and little. If friends weary with travel, should of a sudden come to any of the citizens, and it is not their pleasure to wait fasting till fresh food is bought and cooked and till servants bring water for hands and bread, they hasten to the river bank, and there all things desirable are ready to their hand.*
>
> —William Fitz Stephen, twelfth-century London writer

Street entertainment made up for London's jarring sounds and smells. On the day before Lent, schoolboys engaged their roosters in cockfights, and men young and old enjoyed games of street football (known as soccer in the United States).

boats while one passenger aimed a lance, or spear, at a floating target. Guilds (groups of craftspeople) presented outdoor plays based on Bible stories. The guild of the shipwrights, or shipbuilders, performed plays about Noah. They had great fun by acting out scenes of Noah having arguments with his wife. They used their boatbuilding skills to make models of the Ark.

In the summer, people took up sports like archery, wrestling, stone throwing, and javelin slinging. Girls held dances in the light of the rising moon. Londoners headed to surrounding fields to hunt and hawk or simply to walk past water-powered mills beside flowing streams. As the weather turned cold, Londoners bet on fights between a pack of dogs and a bear or bull. When the marshes froze, children and a few adventurous adults strapped shinbones from animals to their shoes and used spiked poles to scoot themselves across the ice.

A London House

As London grew in population, homes grew upward. They rose to two, three, even five stories. To make more living space, each level of a house extended farther toward the street than the one below it. These homes were built of wood frames that workers hewed, or cut and shaped, outside of the city and brought in by boat. Once the timber frames were raised, the floors and roofs were built and the walls were filled in with wattle (split branches woven together) and covered with daub (mud or plaster).

Craftspeople lived in the attics above their shops or in the cellars below. (Though damp, cellars were relatively warm in the winter.) Thatched, or straw, roofs kept the heat in and the rain out. Early homes had no fireplaces, just a fire in the middle of the room with vents in the roof. In some homes, an arched beehive oven was built into the corner and used for baking bread.

Winter winds often took their toll on such homes. A gale in 1090 knocked down six hundred wooden houses, leaving their occupants destitute. Worst of all, fires broke out on an almost daily basis, often engulfing whole neighborhoods. The threat became so grave that in 1189, King Richard I decreed that the first floor of every home must be built of stone, and roofs must be covered with slate or tile. Unfortunately the law was poorly enforced, and fire remained a threat throughout much of London's history.

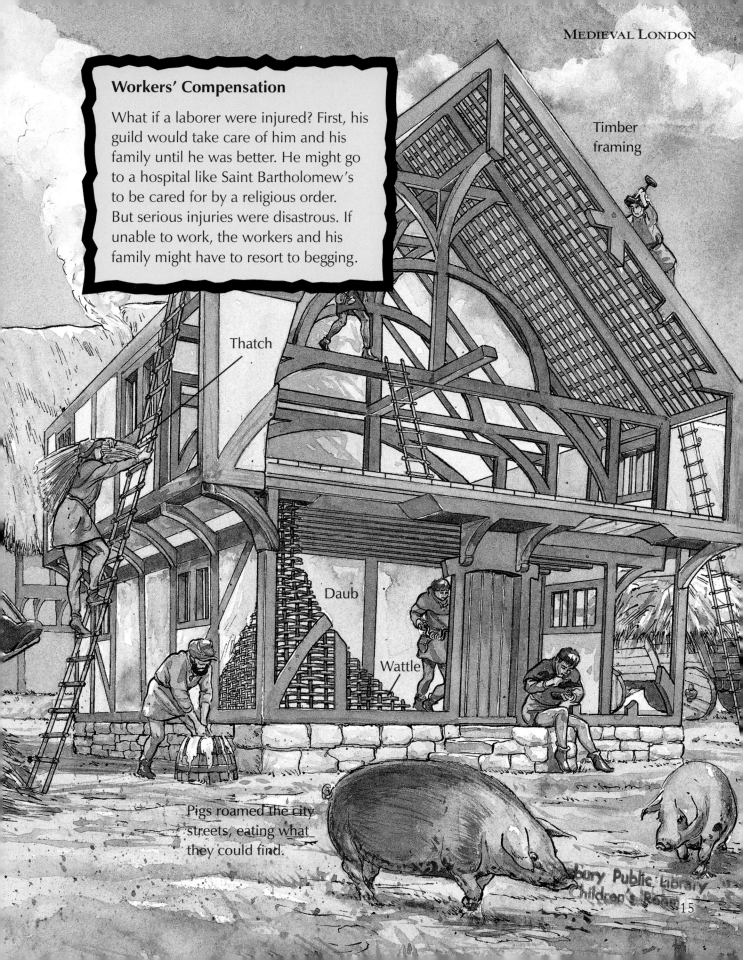

Workers' Compensation

What if a laborer were injured? First, his guild would take care of him and his family until he was better. He might go to a hospital like Saint Bartholomew's to be cared for by a religious order. But serious injuries were disastrous. If unable to work, the workers and his family might have to resort to begging.

Timber framing

Thatch

Daub

Wattle

Pigs roamed the city streets, eating what they could find.

15

The Year Round

The work week lasted Monday through Saturday, a routine broken by markets held on Wednesday and Saturday mornings. Washing day was Saturday, which was also the best day to go to socialize. By law, people had to attend church on Sundays. Taverns stayed closed, and the afternoon was reserved for religious instruction or quiet games.

Each month had one or two major holidays when people could put down their tools and celebrate. Most London holidays commemorated a religious event, and church attendance was required. January 1 marked the Circumcision of Christ, when people exchanged gifts of apples, oranges, eggs, nutmegs, or gloves. On Epiphany, the twelfth day after Christmas, people shared a spiced fruitcake containing a dried bean and a dried pea. The one whose piece held the bean was called Lord of Misrule and the holder of the pea was Queen.

On January 25, the Conversion of Saint Paul, people watched the sky for signs that foretold what the coming year would bring. A clear sky predicted a good year, a windy day foretold war, and a cloudy day promised plague. On Shrove Tuesday, the day before Lent, people feasted and played games. In one such game, called Cockshy, a rooster was tied to a stake. Participants threw sticks at the rooster from a set distance. If they knocked over the rooster and could run and pick up the stick before he got up, they won.

In May, during the feast of the apostles Philip and James the Younger, everyone looked forward to the arrival of summer. It was a day when a young couple could dally in the woods and gather flowers. To celebrate the wheat harvest, people exchanged seedcakes.

Each year ended with Christmas and twelve days of dancing, indoor games, and folk plays. Holly, ivy, bay leaves, rosemary, and mistletoe decorated the homes of London.

Although Londoners worked hard, long weeks, they also knew
how to celebrate with activities like the Morris Dance (*facing page*)
or jousting tournaments featuring knights on horseback (*above*).

Saint Paul's Cross

*I*n the days before many books or any newspapers existed, public preaching was highly popular and often a way of getting the latest news. Every town or village near London had a preacher's cross, where visiting friars would stop and give a sermon.

Saint Paul's Cross in London was one of the most important religious sites in the city. Preaching was a major form of entertainment as well as of religious teaching—great preachers were considered celebrities.

If people liked what they heard, they expressed their agreement with a tuneless humming sound. Sometimes it got so boisterous that the preacher had to step back and wait for the humming to settle down. When people heard the preachers freely express thoughts and beliefs, they were encouraged to do the same. Advances in printing made written resources more available and accessible, such as an English translation of the Bible. (Previously the Bible had been translated only into Latin.)

This access to information helped further religious and political discussion. In London, this freedom of thought and expression sometimes got out of hand. In the Evil May Riots of 1517, a preacher urged a group of apprentices to attack foreigners. Officials overreacted, firing off the cannons in the Tower of London and sending in troops, who took four hundred prisoners. The mob leaders were hanged and their bodies drawn (disembowled) and quartered (pulled apart by horses)—the usual rough justice of the time.

Sermons at Saint Paul's Cross *(right)* could last for hours. Members of the royal party attended as well as common folk. Around the edges of the crowd, dogcatchers kept hounds from disrupting the proceedings. Street vendors offered refreshments.

18

London Bridge

The Romans were the first to cross the Thames River using a slender wooden bridge. For hundreds of years, wooden bridges were repeatedly destroyed by fire and rot. Medieval architect Peter de Colechurch was hired to oversee the building of a stone bridge. For a foundation, workers pounded large supporting pillars into the riverbed. Dangerous river tides caused the deaths of one hundred and fifty workers. It took more than thirty years to complete the bridge. Colechurch himself died four years before the project was complete and was buried in an unfinished chapel near the center of the bridge.

By the time Queen Elizabeth I came

Heads of executed prisoners on spikes

Southwark Gatehouse

to the throne in 1558, the bridge was filled with houses and stores. The shops on the bridge were known for their clothing and household goods. The street was filled with shouting vendors selling their wares, horses clip-clopping across cobblestones, and church bells calling out the time every fifteen minutes. The grisly heads of executed traitors were set on spikes at the entrance to the bridge.

A cage and stocks (wooden restraints for hands and feet) held prisoners bound for the local jail.

Passing by boat under the bridge took courage. The starlings, or pylons on which the arches of the bridge sat, created wild rapids when the tide came in or out. These rapids had to be carefully navigated. Roughly two thousand watermen braved the rapids and rowed the small boats that were the taxis of their day.

Starlings

Rapids created by tides

> I like silk stockings well, because they are pleasant, fine and delicate, and henceforth I shall wear no more cloth stockings.
> —Queen Elizabeth I

A Simple Wardrobe

An admirer of Queen Elizabeth I once noted, "If ever any person had either the gift or the style to win the hearts of the people, it was this queen." Inspired by the dramatic clothing of her father, King Henry VIII, Elizabeth I used her wardrobe to show the public that she was every inch a ruler.

At one point in her lifetime, it is said that she owned as many as three thousand dresses. Queen Elizabeth imitated some of the styles of clothing in other countries. She once secretly tried to hire a French dressmaker, even though law required that she use only English garment workers.

Elizabeth's wardrobe was designed to suggest the purity of her unmarried state— she was fond of pearls and prints of spring motifs. Intricately crafted lace was stiffened into wide ruffs, or collars, which she wore around her neck, framing her face.

She delighted in showing off her red hair and pale complexion, popularizing both fiery orange and yellow clothing and heavy white makeup. Her wealthy subjects, looking to gain her favor, sent gifts of richly embroidered cloth to her dressmaker.

The ritual of dressing Queen Elizabeth every morning was elaborate and time-consuming. First, ladies-in-waiting selected a dress from her collection. Elizabeth then put on a long, loose gown made of linen or wool.

The ladies then fit the queen with a stiff garment called a corset, which was fashioned together with a flat piece of bone or wood. The corset created the illusion of a flat stomach, which was fashionable for women in Elizabethan times. Following this, a farthingale, or set of hoops, was placed around her hips to provide support for the wide skirt. It required the efforts of several women to place the gown over these undergarments, position the heavy embroidered fabric, and fasten the back.

While clothing could be relied on to express her position as queen, it was important to Elizabeth that she continue to appear youthful to her subjects. She commissioned many artists to paint her portrait, posing for them in full royal regalia. She also posed in direct sunshine that helped hide her wrinkles and uneven skin tone. Artists did their best to portray the queen as an ageless beauty, even as the woman herself entered old age.

Queen Elizabeth I controlled her public image with portraits designed to disguise her age (facing page).

Theater in London

In 1576 actor James Burbage opened the first playhouse, known as The Theatre. It was built in a rough section of London dotted by taverns and arenas for bearbaiting (setting dogs loose to attack chained bears). Although drama in London during the Renaissance (1500 to 1700) had its roots in religious plays of medieval times, it had become a loud, and occasionally obscene, popular entertainment. Many London citizens frowned on theater and did not attend the plays. Traveling actors were legally considered vagrants and could be arrested. Playhouses were even rumored to spread deadly diseases.

Trumpet blasts summoned the audience to a performance. A theater could hold up to three thousand people. Vendors sold everything from pamphlets to pies to herbal medicines. The audience freely shouted actors off the stage if the play was boring—one reason why the great English playwright William Shakespeare wrote action-packed plays.

Because women were not allowed to be actors in Renaissance London, adolescent boys played female roles. These young men were required to learn how to walk, speak, sing, and dance as if they were women. But when they grew older and their voices deepened, their careers ended.

At the Globe Theatre *(right and inset)*, wealthy patrons sat in box seats purchased for a sixpence. Poorer people, known as "groundlings" or "penny stinkers," were forced to stand on the ground near the stage.

A Renaissance Woman

A typical middle-class woman in Renaissance London awoke at dawn in her loose shirt and sleeping cap. After pulling on outer clothes, she rushed through the chilly morning, building a fire and preparing breakfast for family members, boarders, and apprentices living in the home.

Later in the day, she gave lessons to her young children. Only 10 percent of the women at that time could read and write, so these lessons were often limited to teaching manners and household skills.

The noon dinner was usually the largest meal of the day. Typically, the woman prepared and served heavy wheat bread and a thick meat or fish stew. A woman was also responsible for making soap out of lye, a liquid made from firewood ashes. She completed many other household chores, such as trimming the wicks of candles, gathering water from public wells, and changing the straw that cushioned the floor of the home.

Women's work was not confined to domestic chores. In many homes, the ground floor was a workshop. A woman often helped finish leather goods, file pewter, or keep track of the goods produced by her craftsman husband.

The children in the family assisted in the workshop as well, their jobs getting more complex as they got older. It was important for a woman to learn her husband's trade, for if he died, she would likely inherit his business.

Household water was fetched from wells.

Meals were crowded with apprentices, boarders, and family members.

Fish stew

"Bring Out Your Dead!"

In the middle of the seventeenth century, two disastrous events were in store for London: a great plague and a great fire. Conditions were ripe for both. The population of London had grown rapidly to more than four hundred thousand people. Houses were overcrowded, and garbage and sewage filled the streets. Coal smoke filled the air, covering the city in a choking fog.

The Great Plague began in the winter of 1664. Rats from ships in the harbor carried fleas that spread the disease among the people. Victims often died within hours. As the plague took hold, officials found it impossible to keep up with burials. Eventually, people went out with carts to gather bodies at night, ringing bells and calling, "Bring out your dead!" Thousands were buried in mass graves.

People did all they could to protect themselves. To disinfect money used for payment, shopkeepers made customers drop their coins into bowls of vinegar. Dogs and cats, thought to carry the disease, were killed. That turned out to be a mistake because no predators were left to kill the plague-bearing rats. Those who could afford it, including some doctors and priests, fled the city. They were not welcomed back when the plague was over. In all, nearly one-third of London's population died.

Smoke from coal fires was thought to keep the plague away.

Fleas on rats carried the plague.

A British naval officer named Samuel Pepys wrote in his diary that he bought a roll of tobacco to chew and sniff as a defense against plague. Peddlers sold charms with the word *abracadabra* repeatedly inscribed within an upside-down triangle. One innkeeper found a purse of money in the street. Before he would touch the money, he singed the purse with gunpowder, burned it with hot tongs, and then dumped the coins into a bucket of water.

Doctors wore masks to avoid catching the plague.

London Burned Like Rotten Sticks

As London grew, more and more houses crowded onto streets. Because most of the houses were made of wood, fires were a daily event in London. But no fire was as destructive—or so completely changed the face of the city—as the Great Fire of 1666.

It began the night of September 2 in a baker's house. It started out as an ordinary house fire, but the summer had been dry and winds were strong. Dry wooden houses nearby burst into flames. The fire spread quickly during the windy night and was soon out of control. People fled to the Thames River for safety.

Londoners tried using buckets of water to put out the fire, but these "bucket brigades" were unsuccessful. The lead roofs of churches melted and poured into the streets. In all, more than thirteen thousand homes were destroyed, and more than two hundred thousand people were left homeless. The wreckage smoldered for months.

Although a great tragedy, the huge fire had some positive results. King Charles II proclaimed that streets be made wider and buildings be built only of brick or stone. The innovative architect Christopher Wren designed beautiful new churches, including Saint Paul's Cathedral. In these ways, the fire gave London a fresh start.

Siphons to squirt water did little good.

To make a firebreak, houses were pulled down or blown up.

As the fire grew out of control, the Lord Mayor of London was frantic, crying, "Lord! What can I do? I am spent!" The Great Fire did spread quickly. But by tearing down rows of houses—creating a firebreak, where there was nothing to burn—the citizens of London managed to stop the spread of the fire.

31

Cookshop

Drinking shed

Frost Fairs

London Bridge's many narrow arches significantly slowed down the flow of the Thames River. The slower flow of water allowed the river's surface to freeze over in the wintertime. Often the river froze completely, as it did in the winter of 1683–1684. That winter, the ice was so thick that people set up booths from shore to shore, including cookshops, drinking sheds, puppet theaters, and even barbershops.

The Frost Fair was a great excuse to take a vacation and have some fun. Apprentices played soccer. People scooted around on the ice, skating and pulling

Whirligig sleds

London Bridge's arches

Bowling

An entertainer
on stilts

each other in small boats. One industrious printer set up shop on the ice, selling cards that read "Printed on the river of Thames being frozen. In the 36th Year of King Charles II." Fox hunting, ox roasts, and coach races competed for spectators' attention. Frost Fair visitors kept warm munching mince pies and hot baked potatoes. One year, a sudden thaw melted the ice before the stalls could be taken down, plunging them into the river. Frost Fairs continued until 1825, when construction began on a new London Bridge. It let the Thames flow so freely that the river no longer froze over during the winter.

One particular London gang preyed on wealthy gentlemen, threatening to kill them if they were unable to cough up a watch and a handful of change.

Wild Streets

With few street lamps and no police, London was dangerous at night. "Link boys" carried torches to guide travelers through the streets. Some were paid by thieves to lead travelers down dark alleys. The link boys would then extinguish their torches and leave the helpless travelers at the mercy of the robbers. Highwaymen ruled the roads and the parks. Not even members of royalty were safe. King George II, for example, was robbed in his own garden.

Watchmen, also known as charleys, patrolled London's streets at night. Armed with only a lantern and a pole, they kept a lookout for suspicious characters and tried to protect the city's citizens. The first watchmen were unpaid and had a reputation of sleeping on the job. Later, London's watchmen earned a wage and became more aggressive in chasing off would-be muggers and making arrests.

One famous walker of London's wild streets was Samuel Johnson, a writer, scholar, and famous conversationalist. With his young friend James Boswell, he delighted in forming groups made up of men and women who were scientists, actors, writers, lawyers, or clerics—all of whom loved conversation and a good beefsteak. These gatherings often ended in the wee hours of the morning. To keep himself safe while he walked home, Johnson carried a six-foot-long club that he was not afraid to use.

> *Twelve o'clock, look well to your locks, your fire and your light, and so good night.*
> —Watchman's traditional call

Literary London

London quickly picked up Dutch and German printing technology and became a world-famous publishing center, churning out books, magazines, news sheets, and pamphlets. As the industry grew, printers and booksellers clustered on Grub Street. Grub was a place where writers scrounged a living by selling their writing by the line. Some authors became famous, but most were paid poorly. One writer, Samuel Boyse, often had to trade his clothes for food. He was once found penniless, sitting up in bed, wearing only a blanket. Two holes were cut through the blanket so he could write.

Paper was made of cotton or linen rags. Ink came from pine pitch (a black, tarlike substance) and lampblack (soot). Books were made completely by hand—including the paper, the typesetting, and the binding—and were therefore very expensive. Customers would select unbound pages and read them to make sure they liked the book before having it bound.

Signboards for books and other products often used bright pictures to draw in customers. For example, a boot indicated a cobbler (shoemaker), three hats a hatmaker, and a roasting pig a tavern. Sometimes a new business moved under an old sign. One Londoner found a perfume shop under a sign picturing a goat. The signs were framed in iron and very thick. One was so large that it fell into Birde Lane and killed four people.

Samuel Johnson, a writer in the 1700s, strolls London's Fleet Street with his friend James Boswell. Fleet Street, like Grub Street, was one of several neighborhoods where booksellers congregated.

I resolve today to be a true-born Old Englishman. I went into the City to Dolly's Steak-House in Paternoster Row. A beefsteak-house is a most excellent place to dine at. You come in there to a warm, comfortable, large room, where a number of people are sitting at table. You take whatever place you find empty; call for what you like, which you get well and cleverly dressed. My dinner (beef, bread and beer and water) was only a shilling.

—James Boswell

London's Coffeehouses

By 1702 more than five hundred coffeehouses had sprung up in London. Coffee was an expensive luxury, taken with sugar but no milk. Customers could buy unsweetened hot chocolate, too. Inside these coffeehouses, owners offered newspapers and tacked up interesting letters from faraway places. But more important was the exchange of ideas among people with similar interests. Each coffeehouse attracted people from a specific walk of life. "Old Man's" and "Jonathan's" attracted stockbrokers. "Will's Coffee

Penny for Your Thoughts

Home to artists, bankers and intellectuals, coffeehouses were brimming with the exchange of new ideas and opinions. Because of this, London's coffeehouses were widely known across the country as "penny universities." It was said that a person could learn more practical knowledge at a coffeehouse than by studying from books for an entire month. In those days, a cup of coffee cost just one penny.

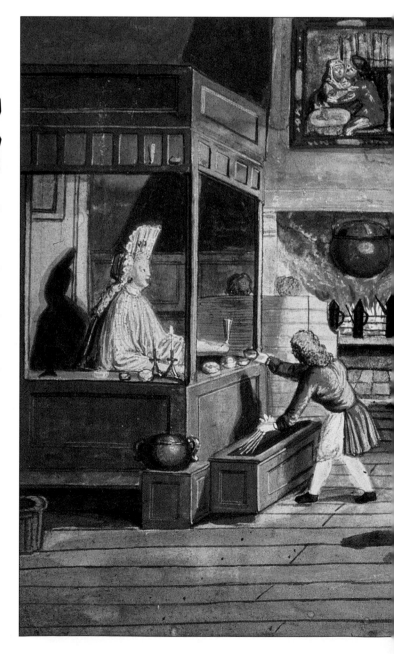

London's coffeehouses were cozy havens where people could conduct business and exchange ideas.

House" was the haunt of writers. The "Cocoa Tree" catered to politicians. "The Little Devil" attracted military officers. "Lloyd's" was a hangout for shipowners and insurers—it later became a world-famous insurance house.

Coffee was most likely brought to England after travelers reported on the dark, syrupy drink they tried in Middle Eastern countries. Although Venice, Italy, received Europe's first shipment of coffee, it was the English who made drinking coffee a popular leisure activity.

Coffee drinking continued to prevail across England until the cost to import coffee became too high. As a result, Londoners switched to drinking tea, which was imported at a lower cost.

River and Sea

By the eighteenth century, one-quarter of London's population depended on the sea in some way. These included fishers in their small, round leather-covered coracles (boats), fishmongers selling fish, stevedores unloading cargo from ships, sailors, custom officials, and watermen.

Over time, London expanded its trade routes. No longer trading with just mainland Europe, London's merchant ships sailed all over the world. By the end of the 1700s, Britain had colonies and merchant ties on every continent except Antarctica.

As trade links grew, raw materials from abroad were brought to London, made into products, and sold. Tobacco processing, sugar refining, silk weaving, and cloth dyeing were important London industries. Tragically, trading also included capturing people and selling them into slavery. London once led the Atlantic slave trade, sending more than one hundred thousand Africans to the West Indies (the islands south of the modern-day United States).

As London's shipping industry grew, the Thames River became overcrowded with trade ships. Ships often had to wait weeks for unloading. In response Londoners built Saint Katherine's Dock, a harbor with guarded, multistory warehouses that kept thieves from taking the cargo. Downriver from London, Greenwich became the navigational center of the world.

By the end of the eighteenth century, the Thames River was overcrowded with oceangoing ships, the lighters (smaller boats) that unloaded them, and barges.

London Builds

London's streets and lanes had changed little from medieval times. The city had grown in a hodgepodge fashion, and the rapid growth of industry had caused it to become polluted. The mixture of coal smoke and fog was so heavy that one visitor found he needed a candle to write a letter at 10:00 A.M. Formerly beautiful sites, such as the elegant Saint James Park in front of Buckingham Palace, were run-down. A visiting German prince thought the park nothing better than a meadow for cows.

Builders came to the rescue. Dr. Nicholas Barbon built affordable row houses, each with its own strip of garden behind. Other builders put up expensive multistory town houses facing crescent-shaped parks or scenic boulevards. The different types of housing soon divided London. New developments attracted the rich, pushing the poor into shabbier neighborhoods.

John Nash was one of the more influential builders. A member of the British royal family hired Nash to design a wide road that would link three London royal residences. Nash drew up a plan for what later became Regent Street, which cuts north-south through the heart of London. The street ended in farmland that was eventually converted into huge Regent's Park. Nash's efforts, and the efforts of others like him, left London with scenic areas and open streets that were right for their times and are still enjoyed by modern Londoners.

Augustus at Rome was for building renown'd
And of marble he left what but brick he found:
But is not our Nash, too, a very great master
He found London brick and leaves it all plaster.
    —Rhyme inspired by some of
    John Nash's cheaply made buildings

> What I left [as] open fields producing hay and corn, I now find covered with streets and squares, and palaces, and churches.
> —Tobias Smollet, author, remarking on London's rapid growth

Piccadilly Street, with its expensive buildings and scenic boulevards, was a dramatic change from the tight, winding lanes that had been the norm in London for centuries.

Conditions for the Poor

As the capital of the worldwide British Empire, London could boast a standard of living higher than anywhere else in the world. Yet thousands lived a hand-to-mouth existence, working in any job that would keep them alive. Children called "mudlarks" wandered along the banks of the Thames, looking for anything they could use or sell. Young chimney sweeps were forced by their employers to climb into chimneys and loosen encrusted soot. Rubbed with salt to toughen their skin, they still suffered constant cuts and scrapes and often died of suffocation while stuck in a chimney. The streets themselves provided a livelihood. "Pure finders" gathered dog droppings and sold them to tanners for the processing of animal hides. Bone pickers, crossing sweepers, and rag gatherers worked in the gutters. Young rat catchers sold their catches to sporting clubs, where bets were placed on how many rats a dog could kill.

One of the more unusual trades involved searching through the sewers of London. With candles attached to their hats and long poles used to test their way,

"toshers" searched underground sewers for coins and metal. They made a better-than-average living, but they faced the perils of attacks by rats, suffocating vapors, and crumbling tunnels. They always worked in pairs so that if danger came, one could help the other.

The poor lived in damp, dark, overcrowded rooms. The very poor resorted to cheap flophouses, where they rented a place along one of the many heavy ropes strung across a large room. They slept with their arms hung over the rope. In the morning, the rope was released, and they tumbled to the floor.

A family with regular work enjoyed bread, potatoes, herring, pickles and onions, and sausages during the week—and perhaps beef or mutton on Sundays. The very poor ate pea soup, baked potatoes, or hot eels from street vendors, or they warmed whatever they could find over a communal fire.

Nothing is known about this man *(inset)* except that he was a matchseller on the streets of London. For many Londoners, cast-off clothing and tumbledown buildings *(right)* were the best they could hope for.

Long Hours

A chair maker worked from 6:00 A.M. to 9:00 or 10:00 P.M., with only ten minutes off for breakfast, twenty minutes for lunch, and eight minutes for tea—and this was done Monday through Saturday and forty Sundays out of every year. A household maid started work at 5:00 A.M. and worked until 8:00 P.M. A shop assistant worked until 10:00 P.M. on weekdays and until midnight on Saturdays.

Elaborate train stations like Charing Cross Station *(above)* were often
built next to luxury hotels. The stations were monuments to a system
of transportation people thought could never be improved.

The Railways

The building of London's railway system marked the beginning of Queen Victoria's reign (1837–1901). The city became a jumble of digging, construction, and demolished housing. Twenty thousand people, mostly residents of low-income housing, were forced to relocate as the tracks were built. The railway companies were required to offer housing options for those who were relocated, but often the new housing was too expensive for those who needed it.

Even without the added visitors arriving by rail, the city was bursting with wagons and streetcars—not to mention the cattle that were still herded down streets to the meat market at Smithfield. Charles Pearson, a surveyor of the city, proposed that London build an underground train line. At first he was ridiculed as impractical, but his idea finally caught on.

The building of the Underground, as the subway came to be known, meant whole sections of streets had to be shut down as great pits were dug and covered over. When the Underground's first cars glided down the track with their one-penny passengers, the city changed forever. London's railways were a great equalizer, allowing both rich and poor to travel throughout the city for a reasonable fare.

The glimpse of the transept [of the Great Exhibition] through the iron gates, the waving palms, flowers, statues, myriads of people filling the galleries and seats around, with the flourish of trumpets as we entered, gave us a sensation which I can never forget, and I felt much moved.... One felt, as so many did whom I have since spoken to—filled with devotion— more so than by any service I have ever heard.
—Queen Victoria

At London's Great Exhibition in 1851, six million people visited the Crystal Palace (*above*) during the 140 days that it was open.

The Great Exhibition

In 1849 Prince Albert, Queen Victoria's husband, proposed an exhibition to display products of the Industrial Age. The architect Joseph Paxton designed a massive building made of glass and iron to be built in Hyde Park. It was known as the Crystal Palace. The revolutionary structure depended on the new railway system to import supplies. People paid five shillings apiece for the privilege of watching the 293,655 panes of glass and 330 iron columns come together.

Before the Great Exhibition opened on May 1, 1851, thousands of ticket holders camped out in Hyde Park. The event showcased one hundred thousand objects, including everything from the absurd, such as a "defensive umbrella" and stuffed squirrels from America, to such technology as the newly invented gas cooking stove and the graphite pencil.

People outside of London used the new train system to reach the Crystal Palace. On days when the admission price was a shilling, members of the working class would visit, while members of the upper class showed off their wealth by waiting for the more expensive days. The Great Exhibition became a symbol of the pride and importance Victorians (those living during Queen Victoria's reign) placed on science and industry.

The Great Stink, 1858

The long hot summer of 1858 brought the poor sanitation of overpopulated London to the public nose. The summer was so dry that much of the water in the Thames evaporated, and the level of the river sank. Sewage dumped into the river was not swept out to sea. The river itself became a stagnant cesspool. Sheets dipped in disinfectant were hung in the windows of Parliament to mask the scent of the Thames.

Because water was not filtered, it was dangerous to drink. Medical officials warned against public drinking fountains, even though the fountains were inscribed with slogans suggesting the health benefits of drinking fresh water. Too many bodies crowded the cemeteries, and rotting carcasses poked through the

The figure of death pumps polluted water at a communal pump (above). The disease-carrying water caused widespread death from cholera. Improved sewage lines and water lines, such as those in the Thames Embankment (right), slowly made London a healthier city.

ground. Pipes passed through these cemeteries, carrying diseased, unfiltered water to London citizens. As a result, cholera, a severe bacterial disease, killed as many as four hundred people a day.

Edwin Chadwick, a social reformer, recognized that inadequate drainage and poor sanitation caused the cholera outbreak. Public bathhouses and laundry facilities were opened to the poor, who would otherwise not have been able to afford using them. Laws were passed requiring freshness and purity in food. Regular garbage collection was established, and graveyards were closed to burials. The tax on soap was abolished to encourage more people to buy and use it.

The city's Metropolitan Board of Works built an expansive drainage system that widened the crowded, trash-filled streets of London. The board also created new riverbanks for the Thames, making space for new pipes to carry sewage downriver.

That great foul city of London—rattling, growling, smoking, stinking—ghastly heap of fermenting brickwork, pouring out poison at every pore….
—John Ruskin, author, art critic

The Edwardians and the Vote

The reign of King Edward VII, from 1901 to 1910, became distinguished by a love of luxury and high society. Members of the upper class devoted their free time to visiting the theater, the opera, and the horse races. Stock-market financiers, American millionaires, and famous actors attended elaborate champagne parties. Meals were taken five times a day and included rich delicacies, such as lobster salad and goose stuffed with small birds. In attending all of these social events, members of the upper class would change clothes up to six times a day.

World War I, which lasted from 1914 to 1918, was a sobering contrast to this time of jolly internationalism. As men went off to become soldiers, women stepped into factory jobs. Their newfound liberty encouraged the growth of the women's suffrage movement, which worked to change the laws and to allow women to vote. Women of all classes banded together and organized rallies, speeches, and fund-raisers. Some of the women, or suffragettes, were known for their militant methods, including smashing windows, defacing works of art, and chaining themselves to government buildings. One woman died when she threw herself in front of the king's horse during a horse race.

Hundreds were sent to jail, where they starved themselves until released. Prisons began to authorize forced feedings. A suffragette handbill described, "I am fed by stomach-tube twice a day. They prise [force] open my mouth with a steel gag, pressing it in where there is a gap in my teeth." Women did not receive the right to vote in Britain until 1929.

> *You have to meet prejudice with sound argument, opposition with hard facts, and indifference with telling points on the present status of the women. Whatever your work in the coming campaign, whether speaking, organizing, or quietly converting friend and foe, you must be ready with the right thing at the right moment.*
> —The newspaper *Votes for Women*

On May 21, 1914, police arrested several suffragettes, who, to draw attention to their cause, had chained themselves to the railings of Buckingham Palace.

The Underground between Aldwych and Holborn *(above)* accommodated Londoners seeking safety from German bombs. Sometimes children slept in hammocks stretched between the rails *(right)*. Some children were later evacuated to the countryside, away from the worst of the bombing.

Blitz Nights

In the beginning of World War II (1939–1945), German bombers targeted only military targets. But on the night of August 20, 1940, German bombers halted their strikes on military targets and unloaded their bombs onto civilian targets. The bombs struck inner London. In one night, the war escalated to include innocent civilians. The Blitz—a sudden aerial raid—had begun. It would continue until May 1941.

Worst hit were the East Enders, working-class people living in the warehouse and factory districts on the eastern side of London. Rumors sprang up that, as usual, the poor were getting the worst of it. Then Buckingham Palace was hit. "Now I feel I can look the East End in the face," said Queen Elizabeth, the wife of King George VI.

Temporary bomb shelters were quickly built, but the locals lost confidence in them. The roof of one shelter fell in when two small boys climbed on top to watch the searchlights. Abandoning the shelters, Londoners hurried to a part of the Underground still under construction. There, hundreds of people huddled through the nights, without heat, water, or sanitation. The idea caught on. Whenever the air-raid sirens went on, people rushed to the Underground stations, sometimes having to ride trains down the line to find open platforms. Once there, they would pull out sandwiches and make the best of it. At least they knew they would live to see another dawn.

Some Londoners built backyard bomb shelters. They settled into a routine, making the shelters as comfortable as possible with bunks, lights, a thermos of coffee, even a bed for the family dog. However, when the "all clear" sounded, smoking rubble was all that remained of some homes. In all, more than thirty thousand Londoners died in the Blitz.

Not all the bombs dropped on London exploded. One, eight feet long and weighing one ton, lodged twenty-eight feet underground near Saint Paul's Cathedral. The officer in charge, Lieutenant James Davies, thought the bomb might be booby-trapped. Instead of defusing it, he loaded the bomb onto a truck and drove it to a marsh near the Thames. When it was set off, the bomb made a crater three hundred feet wide. Some unexploded bombs ended up lodged in walls two stories above the ground. Others landed near natural-gas tanks. Parachuted land mines dangled from trees and streetcar wires, set to go off at the least touch.

A Planned City

World War II ravaged the London landscape and left thousands of Londoners homeless. People were crammed in temporary shelters and abandoned mansions. Many historic churches and buildings were destroyed by the bombings. To provide housing and to raise the public morale, London officials planned a massive rebuilding. On bombed-out sites, workers put up small houses and provided them with tiny garden plots. Crews built fifty thousand new brick apartment complexes and rebuilt shops, churches, and schools in poor neighborhoods. Grassy "Green Belt"

The people of London worked hard to reconstruct their city after World War II. Prefabricated housing was erected on London's East End *(facing page)* to provide shelter for residents who had lost their homes. Workers cleared portions of a building destroyed in the bombing at London's Canon Street *(above)*.

spaces were planted where clusters of old, crumbling buildings had once stood.

Where brick had prevailed, concrete was used in the new structures. This changed the way London looked. Meanwhile the war had drained the British economy, and officials cut corners on materials. As a result, many new buildings were poorly constructed.

In 1951 the city hosted the Festival of Britain, a celebration of the Great Exhibition's one-hundred-year anniversary. Held on the south bank of the Thames River, the festival provided a message of hope and change "to demonstrate to the world the recovery of the United Kingdom from the effects of war in the moral, cultural, spiritual, and material fields." The popular festival attracted ten million visitors.

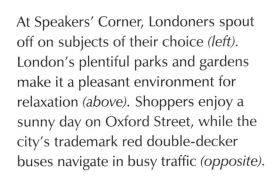

At Speakers' Corner, Londoners spout off on subjects of their choice *(left)*. London's plentiful parks and gardens make it a pleasant environment for relaxation *(above)*. Shoppers enjoy a sunny day on Oxford Street, while the city's trademark red double-decker buses navigate in busy traffic *(opposite)*.

City of Villages

Most areas of modern London are primarily residential. Only a few districts, where daytime businesses dominate, are nearly vacant at night. Londoners of Caribbean, Asian, Indian, and African origin make London an impressively cosmopolitan city. Indian, Lebanese, Greek, and Pakistani restaurants and markets compete with the traditional London pubs (taverns). Still, British pageantry and tradition remain. Daily, thousands flock to watch the changing of the guard at Buckingham Palace or to attempt to get a smile out of the somber horseguards on Whitehall.

Bookstores, publishers, and the headquarters of world-famous newspapers and magazines keep the city's literary history alive. Most people read while riding the clean and efficient Underground system. On Sundays a visitor can hear a fascinating range of freewheeling political and religious opinions (and some creative heckling) at Speakers' Corner in Hyde Park.

London, with its vast museums and intellectual history, is one of the most vibrant cities in the world. While no longer the hub of a worldwide empire, it hasn't forgotten its importance. You may still find postboxes with two slots that read: "London" and "All Other Places."

London Timeline

	First Millennium B.C.	First and Second Millennium A.D.
5000 B.C.–55 B.C **Early History**	**5000 B.C.–2500 B.C.** **2500 B.C.–1600 B.C.** **1600 B.C.–55 B.C.**	Neolithic Britain Early and Middle Bronze Ages Iron Age
55 B.C.–A.D. 450 **Roman London**	**55 B.C.**	Julius Caesar's first expedition to Britain
	A.D. 43	Roman invasion
	A.D. 60	Rebellion of Queen Boudicca and the Iceni nation
	A.D. 200	Wall built around London
	A.D. 409–410	Roman legions leave England
	A.D. 450	Contact between Rome and Britain ends
A.D. 450–A.D. 1500 **Medieval London**	**A.D. 793**	First Viking raids on Britain
	A.D. 1065	Westminster Abbey finished
	A.D. 1066	William the Conqueror crowned
	A.D. 1078	Tower of London construction begins
	A.D. 1176	Stone construction of London Bridge begins
	A.D. 1209	London Bridge finished
	A.D. 1215	Magna Carta signed
	A.D. 1259	Treaty of Paris between France and England established
	A.D. 1362	Parliament opens using English language

Second Millennium A.D.

A.D. 1500–A.D.1700 **Renaissance London**	**A.D. 1517**	Evil May Riots
	A.D. 1558	Accession of Elizabeth I
	A.D. 1576	James Burbage builds The Theatre
	A.D. 1591	First English ship sails to India
	A.D. 1605	Shakespeare writes *King Lear* and *Macbeth*
	A.D. 1613	Globe Theatre burns down
	A.D. 1649	Charles I executed
	A.D. 1659	Samuel Pepys begins his diary
	A.D. 1664	Great Plague begins
	A.D. 1666	Great Fire
	A.D. 1683–1684	Frost Fair held on the frozen Thames River
A.D. 1700–A.D. 1800 **London in the 1700s**	**A.D. 1710**	Saint Paul's Cathedral completed
	A.D. 1753	British Museum founded
	A.D. 1796	Vaccination against smallpox invented
A.D. 1800–A.D. 1900 **London in the 1800s**	**A.D. 1828**	Saint Katherine's Dock finished
	A.D. 1837	Accession of Queen Victoria
	A.D. 1846	First railway station at Euston opens
	A.D. 1851	The Great Exhibition
	A.D. 1858	The Great Stink
	A.D. 1863	Underground opens
	A.D. 1876	Queen Victoria becomes Empress of India
A.D. 1900–present **Modern London**	**A.D. 1901**	Accession of Edward VII
	A.D. 1914–1918	World War I
	A.D. 1929	Women over the age of 21 are allowed to vote
	A.D. 1939–1945	World War II
	A.D. 1940	Winston Churchill becomes prime minister
	A.D. 1951	Festival of Britain
	A.D. 1952	Accession of Elizabeth II
	A.D. 1965	Post Office Tower becomes Britain's tallest structure
	A.D. 1986	M25 (Motorway 25) completely encircles London
	A.D. 1987	Docklands Light Railway opens
	A.D. 1998	The Greater London Authority begins to govern London

Books about England and London

Aliki. *William Shakespeare and the Globe.* New York: HarperCollins, 1999.

Ashy, Ruth. *Elizabethan England.* North Bellmore, NY: Marshall Cavendish Corp., 1999.

Blashfield, Jean F. *England.* Chicago: Children's Press, 1997.

Butterfield, Moira. *The Usborne Book of London.* London: Usborne, 1987.

Ferris, Julie. *Shakespeare's London: A Guide to Shakespeare's London.* New York: Larousse Kingfisher Chambers, 2000.

Fischer, Leonard Everett. *The Tower of London.* New York: Macmillan, 1987.

Green, Robert. *Queen Victoria.* New York: Franklin Watts, 1998.

Green, Robert. *William the Conqueror.* New York: Franklin Watts, 1998.

Hill, Barbara W. *Cooking the English Way.* Minneapolis: Lerner Publications Company, 1982.

Holmes, Burton. *London: The World 100 Years Ago.* New York: Chelsea House, 1997.

Krohn, Katherine. *Princess Diana.* Minneapolis: Lerner Publications Company, 1998.

Nach, James. *England in Pictures.* Minneapolis: Lerner Publications Company, 1990.

Roberts, Jeremy. *King Arthur.* Minneapolis: Lerner Publications Company, 2001.

Severance, John B. *Winston Churchill: Soldier, Statesman, Artist.* New York: Clarion Books, 1996.

Smith, Nigel. *The Houses of Parliament.* Austin, TX: Raintree Steck-Vaughn Publishers, 1997.

Stein, Conrad. *London.* New York: Children's Press, 1996.

Thomas, Jane Resh. *Behind the Mask: The Life of Queen Elizabeth I.* New York: Clarion Books, 1998.

Yancey, Diane. *Life in the Elizabethan Theater.* San Diego: Lucent Books, 1997.

Index

About the Authors and Illustrator

Betony Toht is a writer and editor living in Saint Paul, Minnesota. She has been to London several times and studied there in 1999. Her work has appeared in *Sassy*, the *Utne Reader*, and numerous other magazines. This is her first children's book.

David Toht is a writer and publisher living in Saint Charles, Illinois. A frequent traveler to London, he would rather be on the upper deck of a bus roaming the city than almost anywhere else in the world. He and his wife, Rebecca, have three grown children: two sons, and a daughter, with whom he collaborated on this book. This is his second children's book.

Ray Webb of Woodstock, England, studied art and design at Birmingham Polytechnic in Birmingham, England. A specialist in historical and scientific subjects, his work has been published in Great Britain, the Netherlands, Germany, and the United States. He continues to teach and lecture and especially enjoys introducing young people to illustration as a career opportunity.

Acknowledgments

For quoted material: p. 4, Boswell, James. *Life of Samuel Johnson.* (Chicago: Encyclopedia Brittannica, Inc., 1952); p. 7, Trease, Geoffrey. *London: A Concise History.* (New York: Charles Scribner's Sons, 1975); p. 11, Hibbert, Christopher. *Tower of London.* (New York: Newsweek, 1971); p. 13, Stephen, William Fitz. *Norman London.* (New York: Italica Press, 1990); p. 22, Longford, Elizabeth. *The Oxford Book of Royal Anecdotes.* (Oxford: Oxford University Press, 1989); p. 23, *What Life Was Like in the Realm of Elizabeth.* (Alexandria, VA: Time-Life Books, 1998); p. 25, William Shakespeare. *Henry V.* (New York: Simon and Schuster, 1960); p. 31, Pepys, Samuel, *The Diary of Samuel Pepys.* (New York: Harper & Brothers, 1926); p. 33, Hibbert, Christopher. *London, The Biography of a City.* (New York: Penguin Books, 1977); p. 35, Dodd, A. H. *Elizabethan England.* (New York: G. P. Putnam's Sons, 1961); p. 37, Pottle, Frederick A. *Boswell's London Journal 1762–1763.* (New York: McGraw-Hill Book Company, Inc., 1950); pp. 42–43, Porter, Roy. *London: A Social History.* (Cambridge: Harvard University Press, 1994); p. 48, Hibbert, Christopher. *London, The Biography of a City.* (New York: Penguin Books, 1977); p. 52, Atkinson, Diane. *The Suffragettes in Pictures.* (London: The Museum of London, 1996); p. 52, Atkinson, Diane. *Votes for Women.* (New York: Cambridge University Press, 1983); p. 57, Hibbert, Christopher. *The Story of England.* (London: Phaidon Press Limited, 1992).

For photographs and art reproductions: © Dave Toht, Greenleaf Publishing, pp. 5 (inset), 58; © Doug Armand/Tony Stone Images, p. 5; Mary Evans Picture Library, pp. 12, 34; North Wind Picture Archives, pp. 16, 19, 48–49; Giraudon/Art Resource, NY, p. 17; National Portrait Gallery, London/Superstock, p. 22; Art Resource, NY, p. 24; The Granger Collection, NY, pp. 25, 45, 50; Corbis-Bettmann, pp. 37, 54 (top); Bridgeman Art Library, pp. 38–39; The Stapleton Collection/Bridgeman Art Library, pp. 40–41; Bridgeman Art Library, pp. 42–43; British Museum, p. 44; Hulton Getty/Liaison Agency, pp. 51, 53, 56–57; Coram Foundation, London, UK/Bridgeman Art Library, pp. 46–47; UPI Corbis/Bettmann Newsphotos, p. 54 (bottom); © Andrew Errington, Tony Stone Images, p. 59. Cover: © Doug Armand/Tony Stone Images.